SPONSOR
SUCCESS

A WORKBOOK FOR TURNING GOOD INTENTIONS INTO POSITIVE RESULTS

BOB YOUNGLOVE

Performance Coach

American Literary Press, Inc.
Five Star Special Edition
Baltimore, Maryland

SPONSOR SUCCESS

Library of Congress
Cataloging-in-Publication Data
ISBN 1-56167-736-1

Library of Congress Card Catalog Number:
2002091779

Published by

American Literary Press, Inc.
Five Star Special Edition
8019 Belair Road, Suite 10
Baltimore, Maryland 21236

Manufactured in the United States of America

Dedication

*To the sponsor of my success,
my best friend and marriage partner,
Libby Jean*

ACKNOWLEDGEMENTS

A special thank-you to Kenneth Conklin, Manager for the Meyer Jabara Hotels, whose interest in sponsoring personal and professional performance improvement, inspired this workbook.

To Liz Rayburn, Operations Manager of the Brookshire Suites, and Steve Sharkey, Operations Manager of the Pier 5 Hotel, for their participation in the Sponsorship Project.

With great appreciation for the inspired teaching of Lou Tice, President of the Pacific Institute, and the practical writings of Stephen Covey, Founder of the Covey Foundation.

A personal debt of gratitude to my friends Dr. Tom and Ms. Marti Zizic who have always believed and encouraged me to be successful beyond my own expectations.

To Katherine F. Lewis, my editorial assistant, for her insightful corrections and helpful suggestions.

Table of Contents

What is *SUCCESS* – for You?

Everyone wants to be successful – but how do you define success?

The word *success* comes from the Latin word "successus," meaning outcome or result.

According to Webster's Dictionary, *success* is the achievement of something intended or desired.

However, according to Earl Nightengale, the famous motivational speaker, *success* is not a destination, but the journey toward worthwhile goals.

Another motivational speaker, Matt Oechsli, defines *success* as "the magic in your life felt through disciplined achievement. Commit to the activities that will help you achieve goals, and success will be easy to obtain."

I believe you are successful everyday if you take some positive actions to turn your good intentions into results. You can go to sleep every night feeling successful if you have spent some of your time, talent, and energy doing the things that move you ever closer to your dreams and goals. The personal habits of focused discipline, patient persistence, and hopeful optimism contribute to your success.

Author and speaker Zig Ziglar defines "Total Success as getting more of the things that money will buy, and all of the things that money won't buy." He includes eight elements for total success.

How do you honestly rate your present life condition against these eight elements? On a scale of 1 (low) to 10 (high), how successful are you?

_____Being Happy

_____Feeling Healthy

_____Being Reasonably Prosperous

_____Feeling Secure

_____Having Friends

_____Feeling Peace of Mind

_____Having Good Family Relationships

_____Feeling Hope that the Future will be Better

Balance is essential in becoming a well-rounded person who is experiencing success in all areas of life. Focusing only on success in your career can result in relationship problems, family neglect, and health problems. It is important to focus on goals in all major areas of your life to be truly successful.

Define what would be *success* for you in each of the major areas of your life.

Success in your physical life (health, energy, fitness, etc.) =

_____

_____

Success in your mental life (thinking, knowledge, memory, etc.) =

_____

_____

Success in your spiritual life (faith, values, peace, etc.) =

_____

_____

Success in your personal life (character, satisfaction, etc.) =

_____

_____

Success in your family life (relationships, love, helping, etc.) =

_____

_____

Success in your work life (career, reputation, achievement, etc.) =

_____

_____

Sponsor Success Concept
How individuals can create new habits

WHAT IS SPONSORSHIP:

The Sponsorship Process is a systematic approach for helping individuals improve both professional and personal performance. It is based on several assumptions of human behavior:

1. That most of us take pride in doing a good job of whatever we are doing. Given the choice, we would rather have success than failure, happiness rather than misery, and good health rather than illness or pain.
2. That no matter how good we are doing something, there is always room for improvement. We can always get better at turning our God-given talent into improved performance and surprising results.
3. That we know that we can benefit from some help, and yet we are not always good at asking others for help. Our independence and stubbornness cause us to insist on the "I will do it myself" mentality.
4. That most of us are good at keeping promises to others, but not so good at keeping promises to ourselves. We tend to procrastinate and avoid doing things we know we should do, unless someone holds us accountable.

This sponsor success process takes into account basic human nature and provides strategies for more effectively taking control of your life.

First, it allows you to decide what you want out of life, where you are going, and how you want to live. This workbook helps you define "success" for you. This program does not tell you what to change, but rather helps you decide what you want to change to be healthier, happier, and more successful. If you are perfectly content with your current life situation, your career, your relationships, your health, and if you are confident that this will lead you to where you want to be in 5 or 10 years, then you don't need this program.

Second, this process builds your confidence in your ability to change your behavior and develop the habits that allow you to achieve your goals. It creates new beliefs for you about what is possible and turns your "I can't" into "I can, I will, and I am." This process empowers you to get rid of old habits you don't want and replace them with automatic behaviors that you choose. If you are already perfect, you won't need this program, except maybe to become more humble.

Third, in this process, the help you need comes in the form of a Sponsor who will assist you in being more successful by coaching you in the psychology of behavioral change. This individual will be a trusted friend, a confidante, a mentor, and a coach. You will choose an individual you respect, whom you feel has done a good job of managing his or her own life, someone from whom you are willing to take both advice and encouragement, as well as share your dreams and challenges. Your Sponsor should be as interested in your happiness and success as you are. In turn, you may be a Sponsor for someone you love and care about. If you insist on "do-it-yourself help" and prefer to be a loner, then the workbook may still be of value to you, but you will miss the importance of a coach.

Fourth, this step-by-step process builds momentum toward results. Success breeds success. You can repeat this program over and over again to create many new healthful habits. Once you have learned and applied these strategies in the first six weeks, it will become easier and quicker to repeat the process and increase your results. Besides, you are more likely to accomplish your goals when your Sponsor "holds your feet to the fire" by holding you accountable for doing each chapter and the daily activities. You will learn to keep your promises and commitments to yourself, as well as to your Sponsor. If you are a habitual liar and just can't keep promises to anyone, then even this program will fall short of helping you.

However, if you have dreams, goals, wishes, and wants, then this process of behavior change may be exactly what you need to get moving on making your life all that it can be. Getting yourself a Sponsor, and working together to complete this workbook over the next seven weeks, can and will change your life. The challenge is to turn your good intentions into results. After all, it is not what you know, but what you *do* with what you know that makes a difference in the quality of your life.

A Model for Performance Improvement
<u>The Sponsorship Process</u>
How organizations can get increased performance

The most expensive and valuable resource to the success of an organization is the human resource. Every manager, from team leader and project manager to the organization's vice presidents and CEO, has the awesome responsibility of getting the very best performance from each and every employee. But how do you do this when there is so much untapped potential? Organizations spend mega bucks recruiting and training the very best people. Yet recent surveys have shown that over half of the employees in government and private industry admit that they are in "rustout." That is, on a daily basis, they do not do the very best work they are capable of doing. They are under-utilized in their current positions and are not motivated to perform to the best of their ability. In short, they could do better under the right conditions.

Management's job is to find out what the "right conditions" are and then to help create those conditions wherever possible. The return on investment is a healthier, happier, more successful workforce and organization.

The Sponsorship Process is a natural and logical follow-on to existing efforts to improve employee performance. Take, for example, the dreaded performance evaluation. Once it has been determined what behaviors need to be improved, the Sponsor helps hold the individual accountable for making the change by coaching the employee in how to change behavior, such as how to become more organized, more diplomatically assertive, more innovative, and more capable of handling many priorities at one time. For if you don't know how to change behavior patterns, you believe you can't improve.

Additionally, organizations spend much time and money on training programs to improve job performance. However, the challenge is the transfer of learning from the classroom to the job site. To maximize the value of the existing training classes and learning opportunities, it is necessary to convert classroom knowledge into consistent performance improvement on the job. But this requires changing behaviors, habits, and attitudes, which is not so easily done when we are "creatures of habit." The Sponsor Success workbook should be a natural follow-on for how to turn knowledge and skill into improved performance.

Finally, organizations need the workforce to be flexible and able to adapt to change quickly and effectively in order to continue to be competitive in a global market.

Stephen Covey suggested the <u>7 Habits of Highly Effective People</u>, but he didn't really tell us how to replace old habits with new, more effective ones. Joel Barker's <u>The Power of Vision</u> video convincingly tells us the importance of seeing where we want to be in the future, but not how we have to change today's behavior to get there. Managing back from the future, a strategy suggested by James Belasco in <u>Soaring with the Phoenix</u>, puts us in touch with the need to start changing our behavior now to get better results in the future. In fact, most people already know what they need to change about themselves to be healthier, happier, and more effective in achieving their goals. The question is not *what to change*, but *how to change*.

The Sponsorship Model provides coaching, behavior modeling, and accountability for turning good intentions into results. It starts from the top and cascades down through the organization as a natural function of leadership. The model is based on the principles of self-image change as used effectively in sports psychology, focusing on creating new beliefs and expectations of ourselves at the sub-conscious level of thinking. This new self-concept of "It is like me to..." creates new automatic behaviors that become our habits of success and which move us toward our ideal future.

After all, the #1 responsibility of all individuals is the job of managing their lives, their time, their talent, and their energy to be healthy, happy, and successful in achieving their goals. When the organization they work for takes an active role in helping to sponsor their success, it reaps the benefits in a more self-confident workforce with improved job performance.

Sponsorship Model for Behavior Change
How to master the art of coaching

WHY THE SPONSORSHIP PROCESS WORKS:

Behavior is a combination of *conscious* choice and *sub-conscious* habit. For example, I decide to walk to the other side of the room. Was that behavior *conscious* or *sub-conscious*? It was *conscious* in that I thought about it and made a decision to go to the other side of the room. But was the process of walking *conscious* or *sub-conscious*? It was *sub-conscious* because I did not have to *consciously* think about shifting my weight to my right foot, picking up my left foot, moving my left foot forward, putting my left foot down, shifting my weight to my left foot, then picking up my right foot, moving my right foot forward, and so on. While I was walking, I could even consciously think about other things. What a marvelous mind!

Remember, none of us was born knowing how to walk. We all had to learn how to use our muscles to do this, but through conscious repetition, we have internalized this behavior into an automatic response that does not require conscious effort. Amazing! We can program our sub-conscious minds to do lots of things automatically, like a habit. When we do this, the behavior is natural, effortless, and consistent. It is simply an easier, more lasting way to change behavior so that we do the things we know we need to do to be healthier, happier, and more successful in achieving our goals.

The techniques for programming your sub-conscious mind with the desired behaviors are the same as those used successfully in sports psychology. The process involves affirming new self-expectations, called self-images, that keep us acting in accordance with what we believe is "like us" to do. By choosing the self-image we want, rather than accepting the way we have been in the past, we sub-consciously change our habits. *For example, I used to have a certain pattern I drove home from work each day that became such a habit that I did not have to consciously think about where to turn. When I moved to my new house, I would sometimes find myself in the driveway of my old house. "How did I get here?" I'd ask myself. "I must have been driving on auto pilot." It was time to re-program my sub-conscious pattern.*

The Sponsor Success workbook teaches a variety of methods used to change behaviors and create new habits. Included in the strategies is the use of mental rehearsal or creative visualization that imprints the new desired behavior into our sub-conscious minds. Olympic athletes have been using this technique for years to improve their performance. By adding the process of re-scripting, you can take a failure situation and reformat it to be a success situation next time. We move toward what we picture, so we had better be careful about choosing what we picture in our minds.

Another method is to basically talk ourselves into change. By controlling our self-talk—that is the little voice in our head that comments on our behavior—we can direct our future performance. You see, when you talk to yourself, and we all do, your sub-conscious mind is listening and believes what you tell it. So if you keep saying, "This just isn't my day; nothing I do is working for me" or "I'm so tired I just can't do this," then you're right: you can't! So according to the principle of command, watch what you say, for as you speak, so shall you command.

Sponsorship Model for Performance Improvement
How to help others while helping yourself

HOW THE SPONSORSHIP PROCESS WORKS:

Personal growth and performance improvement, like anything worthwhile, takes belief in achievable results, commitment, and consistent effort. It only takes 4 to 6 weeks to create a new habit, or change an old habit. However, it requires daily focus and practice.

The Sponsor Success Workbook is your personal guide and record of progress. Each week you will learn more about yourself by completing one chapter of activity worksheets. In this way you will learn and apply the secrets of self-image psychological change. Your weekly journal will allow you to reflect on each week's events and let you assess your success at improving your performance through reprogramming your behaviors.

Your Sponsor/Coach is an integral part of the process, both to help you learn the concepts, but also to hold you accountable for using them. Your Sponsor is interested in your success and will meet with you weekly to help you learn the process and share his or her own experience in using this approach to behavior change.

The key to the success of this process is using the FOCUS CARD daily to build a new self-image in your sub-conscious mind that will create a new habit for success. It only takes 5 to 10 minutes each day to change a habit, but it needs to be focused on consistently, every morning and every evening, every morning and every evening, every morning and every evening. By making a commitment and taking it seriously, you will achieve great success.

The Sponsorship Concept
Why do we need help?

Most people are pretty good at keeping promises to others. There is a sense of obligation when you tell a friend that you will definitely do something. There is a sense of commitment to follow through when you tell the boss that this task will be done by a certain time. After all, you are a person of your word and can be trusted to do what you say.

However, when you make those same promises to yourself, somehow you aren't as good at keeping them. Like New Year's resolutions, you soon begin to slack off and make excuses. Worse yet, you accept the excuses. You do not hold yourself accountable for turning your good intentions into results. The word "accountability" can be viewed as "account—ability" or the ability to account for your actions or non-actions.

Therefore, you need a friend, a mentor, a coach to "hold your feet to the fire" and get you to keep your promises to do those things you have chosen to do that will cause you to be healthier, happier, and more successful. This person will help sponsor your success.

Many people are not good at asking for help. Oh sure, if someone asks you to help them, you will do all you can to assist. But ask others to help *you*? I don't think so! Yet the success of this program it greatly increased when you get up the nerve to ask someone to be your coach and sponsor.

What can you expect a sponsor to do to help?

Your sponsor will have an interest in your success. You can share and discuss your dreams, goals, and challenges. As you go through the chapters in this workbook and learn more about yourself, you can discuss the results of the self-assessments and planning sheets. Like a mentor, your Sponsor will share his or her experience and wisdom and offer suggestions. Your Sponsor may help you problem solve roadblocks and make wise decisions. Like a coach, your Sponsor will encourage you to do your very best and may even show you a short-cut or a new strategy. Your Sponsor will hold you accountable for staying on track and being consistent and persistent at working toward success. Like a caring friend, your Sponsor will check up on you, see how you are doing, listen to your complaints, and celebrate your successes.

Selecting the Right Person as Your Sponsor

A key to your success is selecting the right person to be your sponsor and coach. Most importantly, it should be someone you respect and who respects you, someone you trust and are willing to confide in, with the assurance that he or she will honor the confidential nature of this relationship. It should be a person who has a sincere and genuine desire to help you. It is helpful if sponsors are people who have their acts together, are successful at managing their own lives, and have achieved success themselves.

It is nice to choose a friend with whom you are comfortable. However, your best friend may not be the ideal choice, for he or she may accept your excuses for inaction and end up commiserating with your frustrations. You need a person whose authority you will respond to and who can and will hold you accountable.

It helps to have a sponsor who is close by and convenient for meetings and phone calls. The face-to-face interaction is preferable in building a supportive relationship. Although the Sponsorship Process can be done via email and phone calls, it requires more effort.

In selecting the right person as your Sponsor, make a short list of three or four people you think could make a good sponsor for you.

_____   _____

_____   _____

Prioritize your list by comparing each candidate to the qualities described above.

Consider how best to ask the person for help:
You might explain that you have chosen to make some changes in your life and have selected the book SPONSOR SUCCESS: A Workbook for Turning Good Intentions into Results. The book suggests you have a sponsor or coach to help you stay focused and committed to achieve success over the next six weeks. If the person is receptive to the idea, you can send him or her the Job Description for a Sponsor. You might also want to share a copy of the book with that person, so he or she can see what the program includes. Then get together for a meeting to discuss expectations: what you expect of that person, what he or she expects of you, and what you expect of the Sponsor Success program.

Job Description for a Sponsor
In the Sponsor Success Program

The job of a SPONSOR is key to the success of this unique behavioral change program, as published in SPONSOR SUCCESS: A Workbook for Turning Good Intentions Into Results. The secret to the effectiveness of programs like Weight Watchers and The Seven Step Program is the accountability and help provided by others who care about the success of the individual.

A SPONSOR is one who endorses or lends support to a person.

As a SPONSOR of an individual who is choosing to develop new habits that will allow him or her to be healthier, happier, and more successful, your job is to guide, encourage, and hold the person accountable for his or her own success.

Your job is not to tell the individual what to change, but to help that person learn and apply the strategies of how to change behavior and habits to be more successful in achieving goals. It is a combination of the roles of coach, mentor, and friend. Most importantly, it is to help the person stay focused and committed to success.

How much time will be required to be a sponsor for a friend?
About ½ to 1 hour a week for 6 weeks. That time is spent meeting with the person you are sponsoring, helping him or her review the assignments in the workbook, and discussing what he or she is doing to apply the strategies. You may just listen and show your concern, or you may share some of your experience and help problem solve challenges. If you choose to, you can send supportive email messages or encouraging phone messages during the time between meetings.

What are the benefits to you as a sponsor?
You could learn some strategies for increasing your own success. But most importantly, you have the satisfaction of helping someone else become more successful.

I hope you will choose to become a sponsor and make a difference in someone's life. If you have questions or require additional information, you can contact the author, Bob Younglove, by visiting the PATH Associates Web Site at PATHassociatesonline.com.

Motivation, Momentum, Commitment
What will it take for you to be successful?

A desire to improve your health, to be happier, and to achieve greater results in accomplishing your goals. A "burning desire" is a great deal more powerful than just a wish or a want.

A decision to "just do it now" and start today to act in your own best interest. A sense of urgency with a realization you do not have forever to make your life the best it can be.

A dedication to "make time" each week, at least an hour to thoughtfully complete the activities and self-assessments in each chapter. Because you don't have an extra hour, you will have to give up something you have been doing, such as watching TV, and make time to invest in your future.

A determination to select the best person to be your sponsor, coach, mentor, and champion. The willingness to ask for help and accept it. The easiest, most convenient good friend may not be the person who can truly challenge you to be your best, give you honest advice, and hold you accountable for turning your good intentions into results.

The patient persistence to continue to use the focus cards each and every day, twice a day, even when you do not experience a behavior change as quickly as you want or expect. The single greatest factor affecting success is persistence toward your goals.

The sense of satisfaction that comes from knowing that you are doing the things that build success. Enjoy the feeling that you are steadily progressing on a wonderful journey toward your ideal future. The little success will build momentum and commitment to continue the journey, even when the going gets tough.

Chapter One

Determining What You Want to Change

William James declared that the greatest revolution
in his generation was the discovery that human beings,
by changing the inner attitudes of their minds,
can change the outer aspects of their lives.

"Change can be realized through conscious evolution.
Moment by moment, day by day,
concentrate on becoming the person you want to be"

Wilferd A. Peterson, <u>The New Book of the Art of Living</u>

In this chapter:

❑ **Identifying Areas for Self-improvement**

❑ **Qualities and Characteristics for Success**

❑ **Focus on Your Choice of What to Do**

❑ **Your #1 Job – Taking Care of You**

❑ **Behavioral Goal Setting**

❑ **Conditions for Successful Completion of this Program**

Week ONE

Instruction Sheet
Determining What You Want to Change

DATE
COMPLETED

ACTIVITY OR ASSIGNMENT

_____ 1. Complete one or more of the following self-assessments for week one to determine what habits or behaviors you might want to change.

_____ 2. Choose one *professional* behavior, quality, or characteristic that you want to develop in order to be more successful in achieving your work goals. Choose one *personal* habit or behavior you want to change in order to be healthier, happier, and more successful at achieving a personal goal.

_____ 3. Record in your weekly journal specific incidents in which your behavior either helped or hindered you in obtaining your goals.

_____ 4. Choose your Sponsor based on the guidelines for "Selecting the Right Person as Your Sponsor."

_____ 5. Have your first half-hour meeting with your Sponsor to discuss the Conditions for Successful Completion of the Sponsor Success Program and review items 1, 2, 3, (above).

Weekly Journal

SUCCESS I HAVE CREATED THIS WEEK:
(What did I accomplish this week that had a significant positive impact?)

SITUATIONS I FOUND CHALLENGING THIS WEEK:

THINGS I WOULD LIKE TO HAVE DONE BETTER:
(What I learned...)

ACTIONS I PLAN TO TAKE TO BE MORE SUCCESSFUL:

1. _____

2. _____

3. _____

4. _____

5. _____

Identifying Areas for Improvement
What is it you want to change from a personal life standpoint?

WISHES AND GOOD INTENTIONS:
Complete the following sentences with your first thought.

1. I would be more successful at getting what I want in life, if I were more
    _____.

2. I always wished I had the talent and ability to _____.

3. I could achieve my goals more easily if I _____.

4. My personal relationships would be more enjoyable if I
    _____.

5. I would be happier if only I _____.

6. The one thing I wish I could change about me is
    _____.

<u>Identifying Areas for Improvement</u>
What is it you want to change
from a job, career, or professional standpoint?

FROM YOUR MOST RECENT PERFORMANCE APPRAISAL:

What are some of the areas, such as time management or organizational skills, that were identified as qualities or skills that could be improved?

FEEDBACK FROM YOUR BOSS OR FELLOW ASSOCIATES:

Ask others to help you identify areas in which you might perform better in order to be more successful in your job.

TECHNIQUES OR SKILLS THAT YOU LEARNED IN THE TRAINING CLASSES:

What strategies or procedures have you read about or heard about that you would you like to have as a habit or skill?

The Qualities and Characteristics for Success

According to Stephen Covey's #1 best-selling book, *The 7 Habits of Highly Effective People*

1.) **BE PRO-ACTIVE** = *Choose how to act and react to life's situations.*

2.) **BEGIN WITH THE END IN MIND** = *Create a vision of your success.*

3.) **PUT FIRST THINGS FIRST** = *Let your values determine your priorities.*

4.) **THINK WIN-WIN** = *Find ways for each person to get what they want.*

5.) **SEEK FIRST TO UNDERSTAND, THEN TO BE UNDERSTOOD** = *Listen to others before you speak.*

6.) **SYNERGIZE** = *Use creative cooperation to find new ways to solve old problems.*

7.) **SHARPEN THE SAW** = *Practice life-long learning for continuous growth and improvement.*

There are qualities and characteristics essential for your success.
Based on your personal mission, vision of your future, and specific goals,
LIST the qualities and characteristics that you need to develop to be successful.

_____   _____

_____   _____

_____   _____

_____   _____

Focus on the CHOICE of What to DO with
your Time, your Energy, your Talent

Consider the following questions (adapted from the book <u>First Things First</u> by Stephen Covey):

A.)   **What are three activities that you know, if you did superbly well and consistently, would have significant positive results in your *personal life?***

   1.) _____

   2.) _____

   3.) _____

B.)   **What are those activities that you know, if you did superbly well and consistently, would have significant positive results in your *professional career or work life?***

   1.) _____

   2.) _____

   3.) _____

C.)   **If you know these things would make such a significant difference, why are you not doing them now?**

   _____

   _____

   _____

<u>Your # 1 Job</u>
Taking good care of you!

You are responsible for taking the appropriate actions in your life that lead you to *health, happiness, and success.* But how do you define what these things mean to you?   How do you identify your current and long-term needs to be healthy, happy, and successful. What goals do you want to set for yourself in the next six months or year that would result in improved health, greater happiness, and more success?

What does <u>good health</u> mean to you? *For example, fewer headaches, less back pain, more energy to enjoy life after work, less tired in the morning, fewer bouts of indigestion, easier breathing, etc.*

<u>IMPROVED HEALTH</u> = _____

_____

_____

What is happiness to you? What makes you happy? *For example, some time each day to relax and read, listening to your favorite music, taking a walk with a special friend, fewer demands and responsibilities, less conflict, more romance, etc.*

<u>GREATER HAPPINESS</u> = _____

_____

_____

How do you define success? What is it that makes you feel successful in all aspects of your life? Success is not a destination, but a journey toward worthwhile goals. *For example, raising healthy and happy children, maintaining a loving relationship, growing spiritually, helping others, starting my own business, being able to semi-retire at age 50, etc.*

<u>MORE SUCCESS</u> = _____

_____

_____

Behavioral Goal-Setting
Choose two goals to develop new habits

My Good Intentions to Improve:

A.   My Professional Behavioral Goal _____

_____.

B.   My Personal Behavioral Goal _____

_____.

My Current Beliefs about my ability to change:

I believe I can change because _____

_____.

I believe it will be difficult for me to change because _____

_____.

My Current Behavior with Regard to My Goal:

A.   My Habit is to _____

_____.

B.   My Habit is to _____

_____.

Conditions for Successful Completion
of the Sponsor Success Program
*What do you need in order to be successful
in using this approach for
creating new behaviors and habits?*

The Concept

Your Responsibility	To identify and communicate the specific conditions that enable you to achieve success by using your time, talent, and willpower to become the person you want to be.
Sponsor's Responsibility	To work with you to help create, as much as possible, the CONDITIONS under which you are willing and able to consistently apply this method of behavior change.

Success in using this approach = _____

_____

The *Conditions* for my Success

List *the Conditions* under which you would be both willing and able to stick with this program.

Describe *how* these conditions might be created and what you need from your Sponsor and others.

Examples:

Someone to hold me accountable for following the process.	*A Sponsor I respect who will call and meet with me regularly.*
A special time each week to complete a chapter in the Sponsor Success book.	*An hour each Sunday evening to prepare for the upcoming week.*
Ten minutes each morning and evening to focus on my good intentions.	*Get up 10 minutes earlier each day so I am not rushed or hassled.*
Support, not pressure from my family and friends.	*Choose to share this only with people who will be encouraging.*

The *Conditions* for my Success

<u>List</u> the Conditions under which you would be both willing and able to stick with the program.

<u>Describe</u> how these conditions might be created and what you need from your sponsor and others.

Things I need to negotiate with others =

Things I need to change in my daily schedule

Chapter Two

Focus on the Change Process

A transition is a passage or movement from one condition to another. It is the process of development.

*"We move toward what we picture,
and become like the person we imagine ourselves to be."*

Lou Tice, The Pacific Institute

In this chapter:

- ❑ **The Internal Change Process**

- ❑ **Creating a Focus Card for Reprogramming Habits**

- ❑ **How to Determine Readiness for Change**

- ❑ **Effects of Pressure on Performance**

Week Two
Instruction Sheet
Focus on the Change Process

DATE
COMPLETED

ACTIVITY OR ASSIGNMENT

_____   1. Read *The Internal Change Process*.

_____   2. Write out a FOCUS CARD for each of your goals,
                    following steps 1, 2, 3, and 4 of *Reprogramming Your
                    Automatic Response System*.

_____   3. Start using your FOCUS CARDS two times each day,
                    as suggested in step 5 of *Reprogramming Your
                    Automatic Response System*.

_____   4. Record in your weekly journal specific incidents in
                    which your behavior either helped or hindered you
                    in obtaining your goals.

_____   5. Meet with your Sponsor for a half-hour discussion on
                    your FOCUS CARDS and items in your journal.

Weekly Journal

SUCCESS I HAVE CREATED THIS WEEK:
(What did I accomplish this week that had a significant positive impact?)

SITUATIONS I FOUND CHALLENGING THIS WEEK:

THINGS I WOULD LIKE TO HAVE DONE BETTER:
(What I learned...)

ACTIONS I PLAN TO TAKE TO BE MORE SUCCESSFUL:

1. _____
2. _____
3. _____
4. _____
5. _____

The Internal Change Process
for Reprogramming Habits – the Automatic Control System

What is an Automatic Control System?

You cannot consistently act differently than your image of yourself.

Your "self-image" is your picture, or rather many pictures, of you in relationship to specific situations. These pictures are stored in the sub-conscious mind and are based on beliefs you have formed from your past experiences or from what you were told about yourself by others.

When I was a young boy of 4 or 5 years old, I was told constantly by my mother that I was shy. Now, she didn't mean any harm. She just was explaining or labeling my behavior. It happened like this. We would be out at the store and she would meet some of her friends and want me to say hello and shake their hands. I would run behind my mother and hide. She labeled this typical behavior as shy. So I developed a picture of myself as shy, and that image of me kept me acting that way even when I didn't want to be shy.

A self-image is generally expressed in thoughts such as:
"It is like me to..."
"I always..."
"I can't..."
"It is difficult for me..."
The beliefs become the Automatic Control System for keeping us behaving like we think we are.

How Can You Change?

In order to change your old habits, you need to change your old beliefs about yourself into new beliefs about how you can be, how you want to be, and how you are becoming. You need to create new self-images or sub-conscious expectations of your behavior that will guide you in how you automatically behave in certain situations.

In my case, I discovered that being shy resulted in my missing out on a lot of fun things. If I tried not to act shy, I just felt awkward and phony. The opposite of an image of shyness is an image of being friendly and outgoing. So I needed to create a new image for myself, a picture of me being friendly and outgoing. I needed to have a new picture of myself going into a party and walking up to perfect strangers and saying, "Hi, I'm Bob. Glad to meet you."

What do you need to do?

1. Start by controlling your Self-talk

You naturally talk to yourself about your behavior all the time. It is the little voice in your head that says, "I'm good at that" or "I'm always forgetting names." These self-talks are listened to by the sub-conscious mind and help create the self-image. To change your beliefs about what is typical of you, you need to take control of this little voice in your head. You need to repeatedly use positive self-talk statements that affirm the qualities you like about yourself. And most importantly, you need to change the negative self-talk that confirms your bad habits into positive self-talk that describes the way you want to be, rather than the way you have been.

Self-talk statements are:

- ❑ Personal "I" statements. "I choose to...," "It is like me...," "I'm becoming...."
- ❑ Positive statements about what you want, not what you want to avoid. Instead of "I don't feel overwhelmed," say, "I feel in control of my life."
- ❑ Active tense statements that speak about the progress of change toward the goal. "It is becoming easier and easier for me to...."
- ❑ Achievement statements that affirm success, not just intent. Say, "I am..." or "I choose to..." instead of "I can..." or "I will...."

2. Systematically Reprogramming the Self-image

Consistently and repetitively put the new desired self-image into the sub-conscious by saying the positive self-talk and picturing what it would look like when you have that desired behavior. Envision yourself acting with the new quality or characteristic. Repeat this process twice a day for 4 to 6 weeks. This reprogramming process is facilitated by the use of a *focus card* that you will learn how to construct and use on the following pages.

Creating a Focus Card for
Reprogramming Your Automatic Response System

How it's done   **Changing or reshaping your habits is a process of reprogramming your beliefs and expectations about you. As your self-image of you begins to change, so will your automatic behaviors. Your behaviors and habits will change to become consistent with your new self-image.**

Using 3 x 5 index cards or blank note cards, complete the following steps for creating one focus card for your professional goal and one for your personal goal.

Step 1   **List WHAT quality, characteristic, or behavior you chose in Chapter One as your professional and personal goal in order to be more successful.**

top of
the card   *Example*: **More Organized** _____

Step 2   **List WHY it is important to you to make this behavior change. Determine the intensity of your desire to change. List what it will do for you and how it will make you feel.**

Front of   **Know where to quickly find things   Be viewed as competent**
the card

              Stop wasting time looking for things I can't find   Less frustration

Step 3   **Now write a one-sentence description of what your behavior would look like and how it would feel to naturally act in accordance with your new desired habit.**

front of
the card   **I choose to be well organized and put things back where they belong.**

              It is like me to know exactly where everything is.

              It is becoming easier for me to keep track of things and feel in control of my life.

Creating a Focus Card

Step 4   **List any specific behaviors you will need to change to be successful. What will you need to start or stop doing? Write a one-sentence description of yourself doing those things easily, effortlessly, and naturally.**

back of
the card   **I have an efficient system for keeping track of everything.**

I take the time to consistently use my system of organization.

I always put things back where they belong.

There is a place for everything, and everything in its place.

Step 5   **Use the FOCUS CARD everyday to imprint the new image into your sub-conscious mind:**

❑ **Read the focus card, front and back.**

❑ **Close your eyes. Visualize exactly what you're saying and doing.**

❑ **Feel how good it is to have the desired quality and habit.**

❑ **Repeat this process <u>twice each day</u>, first thing in the morning when you wake up and last thing in the evening before going to sleep. Do this everyday, seven days a week, for 4 to 6 weeks, and make the desired behavior a habit.**

Sample Daily Focus Card
Use an Index Card or Blank Note Card

Side 1 = Desired characteristic, behavior, or habit

Step 1

Step 2

Step 3

> *Emotional Control*
>
> *Why important?*
> *Prevent becoming stressed out*
> *Avoid arguments with co-workers*
> *Don't appear rude to guests*
> *Be seen as a competent professional*
>
> *New Image*
> *I rationally choose a calm, professional response to people and situations in order to achieve my goals.*
>   *or*
> *It is becoming easier for me to listen to others with calm, thoughtful consideration.*

Side 2 = Specific behaviors to change or new techniques applied

Step 4

> *New Behaviors*
> 1. *I take a slow, deep breath, pause, and reflect on my conscious intentions and overall goal.*
> 2. *I remain internally calm and respond professionally.*
> 3. *I slow down, sit back, smile, and say, "That's interesting. Tell me more."*
> 4. *I calmly ask non-intimidating questions to better understand the other person's point of view.*
> 5. *I put my own opinions on hold while I focus on what concerns others have at that moment.*
> 6. *I keep a poker face, maintain a soft tone of voice, and speak slowly when expressing my opinion.*

How to Determine Readiness for Change
Are you ready to change your habits?

The Formula of
Key Factors: **(SD + CV + KH) x BIS = C**

SD	=	*Sufficient Dissatisfaction* with the present situation.
CV	=	A *Clear Vision* of the way you want things to be.
KH	=	*Know-How* to do what must be done to change the situation.
BIS	=	A strong *Belief In Self* and the ability to be successful.
C	=	*Choice* and *Commitment* to change.

(adapted from the work of David Glicher)

Questions: Determine your readiness for change. Ask yourself to consider:

My level of dissatisfaction with the current situation;

Ask
- How do I feel about my current effectiveness in achieving my goals?
- Am I satisfied with the present situation and the results I get?
- Do I want things to continue the way they are?

My ability to visualize what I want to be different;

Ask
- How would I like things to be different, better, easier, more effective?
- What would it look like if I were the best I could be?
- How do I want my life, my career, and my relationships to be 6 months from now, or a year from now?

My knowledge of what to do to improve the situation;

Ask
- Do I know what I need to know about how to achieve my goals?
- Am I willing to learn new techniques, skills, and attitudes?
- Do I have any ideas of how I need to change to be more successful?
- Do I know who I can talk to for good advice?

My belief in my own ability and my commitment to success;

Ask
- Do I believe I can change? Will I do it? When? How?
- What is the main reason I haven't done it so far?
- Am I self-confident enough to know I will succeed?

How to calculate your readiness for change:

Use the formula to determine your readiness for <u>a specific change</u> in your life, such as quit smoking, lose weight, start exercising, change jobs, etc.

Use a scale of 1 to 10 for each factor:

1 = very low (i.e., low level of dissatisfaction, no clear vision of the future, no knowledge of how to change, low self-confidence)

10 = very high (i.e., high level of dissatisfaction, a very clear vision of the future, a well thought-out plan, confidence that when you make up your mind to do it, you will succeed)

SD _____ + CV _____ + KH _____ = _____ x BIS _____ = _____
Max score: 10 + 10 + 10 = 30 x 10 = 300

Scoring under 150 indicates that you are probably not ready to change but need to strengthen some factors. To increase your readiness for change, look at the factors having the lowest scores and see what you can do to increase that factor.

Therefore, to increase readiness for change,

I need to increase my dissatisfaction by _____

I need to increase my vision of the future by _____

I need to increase my know-how to do it by _____

I need to increase my self-confidence by _____

For example, the more you fall in love with your dream of your future, the more dissatisfied you become with the present situation, and that builds energy to make a change.

Don't say, "I will try to change, I will try to quit smoking, I will try to lose weight, I will try to exercise." The word TRY implies a lack of self-confidence in your ability to succeed. Don't try! Instead, build your readiness for change so that when you are ready, you know you will be successful. Then instead of trying it, just do it.

Effects of Pressure on Performance
How much stress is too much?

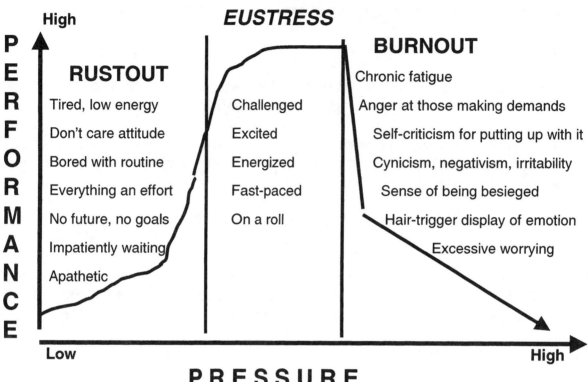

BURNOUT = too much stress and pressure to succeed, causing you to feel overwhelmed, hassled, besieged, and exhausted. You need to get focused and set priorities based on your values. You can't do it all, so learn to let go of the less important things and concentrate on your success.

RUSTOUT = too little pressure or drive to do your very best to achieve success. You are comfortable with the status quo and work to avoid pressure to do more. You need to have a dream and goals that inspire you to take risks and grow to develop your true potential.

EUSTRESS = the right amount of pressure to motivate you to use your time, talent, and skill to be the very best you can be. Sure, there is some stress, but you use the stress to provide energy to accomplish your goals. You are confident and "on a roll" toward greater success.

Chapter Three

Reprogramming Your Habits

A habit is an unconscious inclination to perform some act acquired through its frequent repetition.

"Change requires the substituting of new habits for old. You mold your character and your future by your thoughts and acts."

Wilferd A. Peterson, <u>The New Book of the Art of Living</u>

<u>In this chapter:</u>

- ❑ **How Behavior Patterns and Habits are Formed**

- ❑ **Reprogramming Your Habits**

- ❑ **Systematic Mental Rehearsal**

- ❑ **Creating a Positive Self-Expectation**

- ❑ **Re-framing Your Thoughts**

- ❑ **Re-scripting Situations**

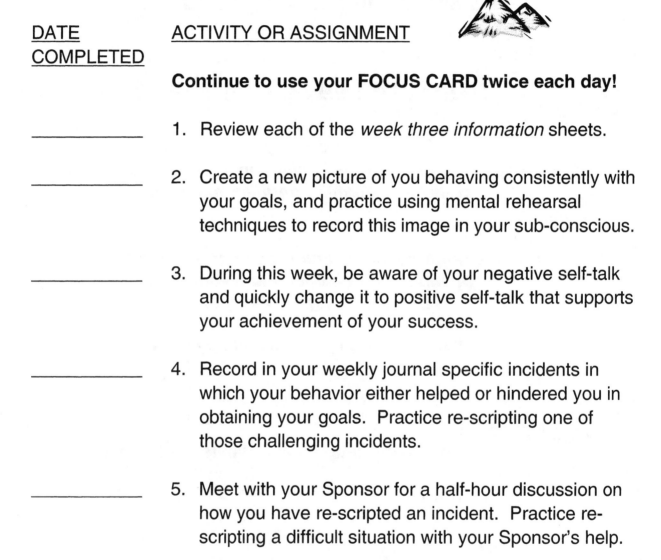

Week Three
Instruction Sheet
Reprogramming Your Habits

<u>DATE COMPLETED</u>

<u>ACTIVITY OR ASSIGNMENT</u>

Continue to use your FOCUS CARD twice each day!

_____ 1. Review each of the *week three information* sheets.

_____ 2. Create a new picture of you behaving consistently with your goals, and practice using mental rehearsal techniques to record this image in your sub-conscious.

_____ 3. During this week, be aware of your negative self-talk and quickly change it to positive self-talk that supports your achievement of your success.

_____ 4. Record in your weekly journal specific incidents in which your behavior either helped or hindered you in obtaining your goals. Practice re-scripting one of those challenging incidents.

_____ 5. Meet with your Sponsor for a half-hour discussion on how you have re-scripted an incident. Practice re-scripting a difficult situation with your Sponsor's help.

Weekly Journal

> **SUCCESS I HAVE CREATED THIS WEEK:**
> *(What did I accomplish this week that had a significant positive impact?)*

> **SITUATIONS I FOUND CHALLENGING THIS WEEK:**

> **THINGS I WOULD LIKE TO HAVE DONE BETTER:**
> *(What I learned...)*

ACTIONS I PLAN TO TAKE TO BE MORE SUCCESSFUL:

1. _____
2. _____
3. _____
4. _____
5. _____

How Behavior Patterns and Habits are Formed
Acting to meet our needs and wants

Most all of behavior is purposeful. Our behavior is intended to satisfy needs and wants, such as the need for food, for excitement, for recognition, for love, etc. When needs are unmet, they create a psychological tension that directs and motivates behavior to satisfy those needs. When you are hungry, you start looking for food. Sometimes, when you don't know why you have behaved a certain way, it is because you are unaware of the basic needs driving your behavior. So in that sense, behavior is not random or accidental, but intentional. To better understand your patterns of behavior or habits, it is helpful to consider the following process.

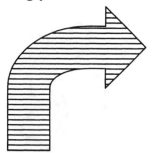

2. CHOICE of ACTION
  * Options
  * Experience
  * Values

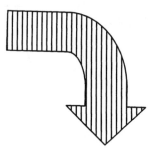

1. NEEDS & WANTS
  * Survival needs
  * Pleasurable wants

3. REWARDS
  * Satisfied needs
  * Reduced tension
  * Good feelings

Example:

#1   You have basic <u>needs</u> for food.
       You also have strong <u>wants</u> for a hot fudge sundae.

#2   Unmet needs create a kind of psychological tension that direct your
       thoughts and motivate your <u>actions</u> to satisfy the unmet need.
  - In choosing the appropriate behavior, you consider your <u>options</u> or
    what you can do to get a hot fudge sundae.
  - Your experience tells you the likelihood of success of each option.
  - Your values tell you whether or not it is okay to act that way to satisfy
    your needs.

#3   The outcome of your actions determines you level of satisfaction.
       Was the craving for a hot fudge sundae reduced? Do you feel good?

For example: One of my first cases when I was working as a Juvenile Counselor taught me the importance of understanding the needs behind the behavior, particularly if you are going to change behavior. Randy was 14 years old and had been referred to me by the police after several incidents of shoplifting. The normal procedure was to scare the kid into becoming a law-abiding citizen or hoping he got good enough at stealing that he didn't get caught. Normally I would have simply explained that the consequences of continued shoplifting would earn him a trip to reform school, and that would motivate him to stop breaking the law.

However, I noticed a pattern to his life of crime. Each time he was caught shoplifting, he had been stealing from a grocery store, and he had always stolen food. Could hunger be the motivating factor? So I went to visit him at home, only to discover he was living alone in an apartment that did not have any food or appliances in the kitchen. He reluctantly told me that his mother was in the hospital with another nervous breakdown, and he had never known his father. He insisted he was doing just fine and didn't need any help. "But when you get hungry, what do you do for food?" I asked. Randy replied, "I steal it, because the stores charge too much and they are ripping the public off, so they owe it to me. Only sometimes I get caught."

His legitimate need led to a poor choice of behavior to meet the need. So what options does Randy have to satisfy his hunger need? He could beg for food, mooch off his friends, go to a soup kitchen, get a job, become a farmer, or steal food. The decision of which option to choose was based on his awareness that the option existed, his belief that an option would actually work to meet his needs, and his sense of values that told him what was okay or not okay. Randy explained that he would never stoop so low as to beg for food, that he was too proud to mooch off of his school friends, that he didn't know of any soup kitchens, that he had tried to get a job but was only 14 years old and needed a work permit, and he knew it took forever to grow food. So stealing was his behavior of choice.

As his Probation Officer, I was responsible for getting Randy to stop stealing. I decided to give him a positive experience with some new options that would satisfy his hunger need. First, I invited him to lunch. We went to a soup kitchen run by a church in his neighborhood. He protested that he didn't want to go anyplace where they preached at you. I said, "Try it once and see." Much to his surprise, the people were friendly, the food was good, and some of the older kids from his school were eating there. "That's not so bad in a pinch," he commented, "but I wouldn't want to make a habit of it."

Next I helped him complete the forms to get a work permit. I then went with him to a couple of restaurants in his neighborhood, and he got hired as a dishwasher. He got paid, and more importantly, he got to take home as much food as he wanted.

41

A couple of weeks later, I went to Randy's home to check up on him. His mother was home from the hospital, and Randy was bragging about being the man of house and bringing home the food. He had not only learned to satisfy his hunger need, but had discovered how to meet his need for personal pride and respect.

What needs or wants do you have? How are you choosing behaviors to meet those needs? When you find a behavior to satisfy your unmet needs and wants, and it works for you, then you are likely to follow the same course of action the next time the need surfaces. And this becomes a habit. If you are going to change some of your old habits, it might be important to consider the following:

1. What is the need or want motivating your behavior?
   What are the feelings you have?
   What is important to you that is not satisfied?
2. What are your choices of behaviors or actions to meet that need?
   a. What new options do you have that you haven't considered?
   b. What has been your experience with those options?
      Do you believe it is a viable option that will work?
      How can you create a positive experience with a new option?
   c. What is your sense of right or wrong about the behavior?
      Do you approve of your behavior, or disapprove?
      Is your behavior consistent with your values?
3. Does your choice of behavior satisfy your need or want and cause you to feel good about yourself?

Discover the reasons for some of your habits.

Your needs & wants	Your choice of behavior	Your rewards

<u>Reprogramming Your Habits</u>

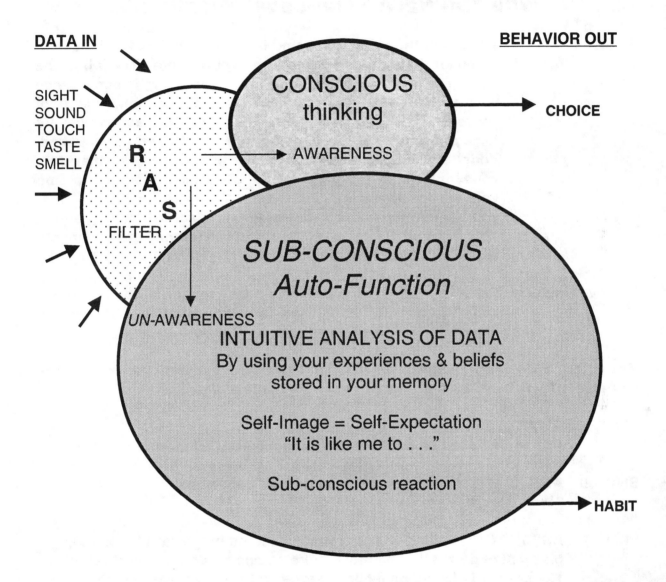

The <u>INTUITIVE</u> Process

We can only understand the present situation in terms of our knowledge and experience stored in our memory.

That analysis defines the situation.

The self-image tells us how to automatically behave in similar situations.

Thus, we act as our habits tell us to, not always as we could choose to act.

The Marvelous Mind
Why You Have a Gut-Level Reaction?

Behavior   The job of the conscious mind is to think and make choices of behavior that you determine to be appropriate. The job of the sub-conscious self-image is to keep you acting in accordance with your beliefs and expectations. So, if your image of yourself is "I lose my temper easily," then the sub-conscious tells you to get angry whenever your hot button gets pushed. Your conscious mind can sometimes override the sub-conscious habit by grabbing the steering wheel and forcing yourself to stay calm. But eventually the autopilot will steer you back to the course your program is set for: getting angry. You see, you cannot consistently act differently than your self-image for any length of time.

Intuitive Analysis   Sensory data, such as sight, sound, touch, taste, and smell, come into your brain and are immediately analyzed to determine their meaning and significance.

Example: You return home from work and walk in the door to your home. Immediately you smell something, something strange and different.

Step 1.   AWARENESS = What is it? *"Smoke"*
Answer is based on experiences stored in your memory.

Step 2.   ASSOCIATION = What have I experienced before that is like this?
"Where there is smoke, there is fire!"

Step 3.   ASSUMPTION = What is this probably leading me toward? Something pleasant or something painful? *"Fire equals destruction and pain!"*
The answer is based on feelings stored with the old memory.

Step 4.   ACTION = How do I usually act in this situation? *"It is like me to find out where the smoke is coming from and call for help."*
The actions are a result of programmed response.

All of these steps in the intuitive analysis process take only a fraction of a second to happen. Because it takes place at the sub-conscious level of your mind, you are generally unaware of the thoughts, memories, and associations. All you are aware of is your gut-level response to respond to the danger.

Systematic Mental Rehearsal
How do you prepare to change a habit?

Mental Rehearsal   Mental Rehearsal is a technique used in Sports Psychology to improve performance. It consists of vividly imagining your precise behavior in a specific situation. The more you rehearse this image in your mind, the more your body will follow that picture. You can use this same strategy to reprogram your sub-conscious habit to have a new automatic behavioral response to a given set of circumstances. Apparently, the sub-conscious mind doesn't know the difference between what actually happens in a situation and what you vividly imagine about it. Therefore, you can train your mind to produce a desired response.

Example: I come home form work tired and stressed out. My children are fooling around at the dinner table and spill some milk. This just ticks me off, and I lose my temper and start yelling at them. They cry. I get angry and send them to their rooms without their supper. Now I have to clean up the mess. No one is happy. So I choose to change my response by practicing mental rehearsal. I create a new picture of how I want to respond in a calm and helpful way when my children fool around at the dinner table and spill something.

In my new picture, my kids are still being kids and fooling around, only this time when they spill something, I see myself remaining calm and I hear myself say, "Oops. Looks like something got spilled. What do we need to do about it? How about one of you get a rag to wipe up the table? One of you get a mop to clean the floor, and someone get some more milk." After all that is settled, I hear myself saying, "So, what do we need to do to prevent this from happening in the future?" (The solution my kids came up with was to put lids on the cups!)

I rehearsed this over and over in my mind until my habit of losing my temper was replaced by calm problem-solving. The result was less stress for me and a much-improved relationship with my children. They no longer were afraid of me; rather, they learned to see me as caring more about them than spilled milk.

The Process   Create a new picture in your mind of how you want to act in a given situation that is consistent with your FOCUS CARD.

Describe what that would look like.   **Describe how you would act.**

Describe what you would say.   **Describe how you would feel.**

Now, practice visualizing the new picture of your desired behavior, over and over again in your mind, until it replaces the old picture.

Creating a Positive Self-Expectation
by Controlling Your Self-Talk

I. Behavior
**I act a certain way
in a particular situation.**

III. Self-Image
**I create a belief about how I usually
act (it is like me to . . .) in this type
of situation. This picture of me tells
me how to act next time.**

II. Self-Talk
**I talk to myself about how I acted
in that situation. I approve (I did
good!) or disapprove (I screwed
up again!).**

Examples of how self-talk controls your behavior:

I. Situation:	II. Self-talk:	III. Self-image:
I am rushing to get to work.	I am always late.	It is like me to be late.
I am late for a meeting.	I never make it on tine.	I always have to rush to
I am hassled and irritable.	I'm always rushing!	to get places.

Create *new self-talk statements* to change your self-image:

"I choose to be an on-time person who gets where I'm going with time to spare"

"I always leave with a little extra time so I arrive calm and confident."

Now, write three self-talk statements that describe the way you would like to be.

1) _____

2) _____

3) _____

Re-framing Your Thoughts
How can you control negative self-talk?

Self-talk   is the little voice inside your head that is constantly chattering away, making comments on your behavior. *"Wow, I'm good at that"* or *"This just isn't my day"* or *"I can't remember names."*

Self-evaluation   of your actions, via self-talk, is listened to by the sub-conscious mind that records the self-talk as fact. Over time, these messages form your image of yourself that tells you how you are and how you behave. *"It is like me to forget people's names."* So you act in accordance with your self-expectation.

Re-framing   is a process of putting a different perspective on the way you see something. By changing the frame on the picture, you make the picture look different. By changing your negative self-talk to positive self-talk, you will learn to have an improved expectation of your behavior. So instead of *"I can't remember names"* you reframe that thought to be *"I'm good at remembering names, and I will remember it in just a few minutes. The information always comes to me."* In this way, you direct your sub-conscious mind to recall the information.

The Process   changes negative self-talk into positive self-talk in order to direct your future behavior:

Instead of "I hate it when this happens," say, "I can deal with this."

Instead of "This really ticks me off," say, "It's not going to ruin my day."

Instead of "I get so angry when...," say, "I'm calm and professional."

Instead of "This is so frustrating," say, "I deal well with challenges."

Now, write new positive self-talks for the negative ones you have been using:

_____

_____

Application   Whenever you catch yourself using negative self-talk, say, *"Stop. I refuse to think this way. The new me is...,"* and use positive self-talk to describe the way you want to be.

47

Re-Scripting Situations
How to act differently next time?

Habits   are the result of learned responses to specific situations that are stored in your memory as self-images. It tells you, "*In this situation, it is like me to...*" and that causes you to automatically behave that way whenever you are faced with a similar situation.

Re-scripting   is a process to change your habits of responding a certain way to a situation or a specific individual by creating a new scenario or script in your sub-conscious mind. By imagining a new ending to the story, *one in which you behave the way you want to, rather than the way you have behaved in the past,* you create a new expectation that is established in your memory.

The Process of Re-scripting:

1. Write down a recent situation in which you did not act the way you would have liked to behave. Analyze what happened, how you felt, and what you said or did.

_____

_____

_____

_____

_____

2. With your Sponsor, review the situation and decide how you would prefer to have acted, what you could have said or done that was more in line with your desired self-image.

_____

_____

_____

__Re-Scripting Situations__

3. **Create a new scenario of how you want to act in that same situation in the future. Describe what it would look like, what you would say, how you would act, and most importantly, how you would feel.**

_____

_____

_____

_____

_____

Imprinting   **is the process of getting the new image in your sub-conscious mind. To do this, practice visualizing the new scenario, over and over again in your mind, until it replaces the old picture with the new expectation of how you will act in that situation.**

Chapter Four

Uncovering Resistance to Change

To work against, fight off, and actively oppose
our forward movement
is to get in our own way by resisting progress.

"Your own dreams, hopes, aims, and purposes mark time
until you start them marching."

Wilferd A. Peterson, The New Book of the Art of Living

In this chapter:

- ❑ **Climate for Successful Performance**

- ❑ **Responsibility for Results**

- ❑ **Expanding Comfort Zones**

- ❑ **Uncovering Resistance to Change**

- ❑ **Turning Good Intentions Into Results**

Week Four Instruction Sheet
Uncovering Resistance to Change

ACTIVITY OR ASSIGNMENT

Continue to use your FOCUS CARD twice each day!

_____   1.   Decide what you need to do to create a better climate for success.

_____   2.   Complete the worksheets *Uncovering Resistance to Change* and *Turning Good Intentions Into Results* for any goals you are struggling with.

_____   3.   Record in your weekly journal specific actions you need to take to increase your success at turning your good intentions into results.

_____   4.   Meet with your Sponsor for a half-hour discussion on the *resisters to change* you have discovered and what you need to do to overcome the resistance.

Weekly Journal

SUCCESS I HAVE CREATED THIS WEEK:
(What did I accomplish this week that had a significant positive impact?)

SITUATIONS I FOUND CHALLENGING THIS WEEK:

THINGS I WOULD LIKE TO HAVE DONE BETTER:
(What I learned...)

ACTIONS I PLAN TO TAKE TO BE MORE SUCCESSFUL:

1. _____
2. _____
3. _____
4. _____
5. _____

Climate for Successful Performance
What do you need from others?

You need certain things from others in order to be successful. You need effective leadership that sets you up to experience success, not failure. Likewise, when you are parenting your children or managing your employees at work, you have a direct effect on other people's performance and success. Words and actions influence others to behave effectively or ineffectively. Creating a climate for good performance must involve the following:

1.) *Understanding of What is Expected*
You must have a clear understanding of others' expectations of you and standards by which they will measure your success.

2.) *Opportunity to Perform*
You must be given the resources, the time, the tools, and the knowledge to successfully meet the standards of performance.

3.) *Feedback and a Sense of Progress Toward the Goals*
You must be provided with ongoing, specific feedback about what is working well and what needs to be changed to achieve the goals on-time in a quality manner.

4.) *Help to Learn and Improve*
You need prompt response to requests for guidance and assistance. Quality coaching should be available to help you learn and develop the skills to improve your level of performance.

5.) *Rewards*
You need to feel proud of your accomplishments and have someone with whom to celebrate your success. Being recognized and rewarded for your good work will build your self-confidence.

Responsibility for Results
Are you respond - able?

Are you able to respond in ways that move you toward your goals of increased health, greater happiness, and more success? Do you hold yourself responsible for the results, or do you blame others for being stressed out, depressed, and frustrated? Are you accountable, that is, able to account for the current conditions of your life, what you have done or haven't done to be healthy, happy, and successful?

When you stop to think about it, no one else is responsible for you, but you. It is not the responsibility of your parents, your boss, your spouse, or your friends to get you to behave in ways that create health, happiness, and success.

Stop expecting your doctor to fix your medical problems without your help in changing the bad habits that may have caused or contributed to them. How about stop smoking and start the habit of regular, adequate exercise?

Stop wishing your family and friends would do things to make you happy. No one can make you happy, or for that matter, unhappy, unless you let them. Happiness is a choice of how you feel in response to what you think about. You can choose the habit of being happy, in spite of the situation.

Stop hoping your boss will reduce your stress level, make your job easier, and offer you a great promotion, without being willing to learn new skills and demonstrate competence and excellence. You manage your career, not the organization you work for. Don't sit around waiting for a promotion; make opportunities for your career to advance.

So what will you do? What responsible actions will you take to move you toward your goals of health, happiness, and success?

To be healthier, I choose to _____

To be happier, I choose to _____

To be more successful, I choose to _____

_____

Expanding Comfort Zones
How to do things you are uncomfortable doing

THE PROCESS FOR EXPANDING YOUR COMFORT ZONE:
Take yourself to <u>the edge</u> of your COMFORT ZONE and be willing to endure a little discomfort, while ensuring that your overall experience is a positive one. That wasn't so bad. A successful experience with the new behavior will build pride and confidence in your growth.

PANIC ZONE
overwhelmed

↑ **Area for confidence and growth**

COMFORT ZONE

feel competent to handle situation; expectations are met

↓ **Area for patience and tolerance**

DRONE ZONE
bored

Three things I could do to expand my comfort zone for change:

1. _____

2. _____

3. _____

Uncovering Resistance to Change

You have been using your FOCUS CARDS for several weeks now, every morning and every evening, to re-program your sub-conscious self-image. You should be feeling some difference in your beliefs about what it is like you to do. You might be seeing some small changes in behavior. You are probably more aware when your daily habit or action is not consistent with what you have been telling yourself about the "new you." Well, this is normal. Changing habits is a process that usually takes 4 to 6 weeks, depending on the strength of the old habit you are changing.

It is time, however, to get out of your own way and stop resisting change. This effort to *Uncover Resistance* is based on the fact that although you may have good reasons *why you want to change*, you also may have good reasons *why you are resisting change*. It's kind of like pushing and pulling on a door at the same time. It is difficult to make progress. Often you may be unaware of how you are resisting, since those beliefs may be hidden in your memory or seem unrelated. It takes a little detective work to uncover the reasons you won't let yourself be happy, healthy, and successful. Psychologists often call it "fear of success" rather than fear of failure.

Example: I had left my secure government job to start my own business. I desperately wanted and needed this venture to be successful. I thought I was motivated by all the good reasons to make this change. However, until my friend Martha helped me with the following activity, I was unaware of certain beliefs from my childhood that were holding me back. When Martha encouraged me to respond by completing the following sentences with the very first thing that popped into my mind, I blurted out, "If I'm successful in my business, it will ruin my marriage." Where did that thought come from? I guess I remembered my parents commenting on how friends of theirs had gotten a divorce because the husband had become successful in his job at the expense of his family.

Isn't it funny what memories and thoughts are cluttering up our minds? Well, once I discovered that thought and chose to reframe it, I began to experience greater success and an improved relationship with my wife and children.

So give this a try and see what you uncover that might be holding you back.

What?   First state your intention to change. Be specific and complete.

        I want to_____

Why?   Next, list all the reasons why you want to do this and how it will benefit you to make this change. Get in touch with your real motivation.

_____   _____

_____   _____

_____   _____

Why not?   Why haven't you turned your good intentions into results before now? To discover your hidden reasons, quickly complete the following sentences with the first thing that comes into your mind.

The real reason I haven't done it is_____

_____

I would if only_____

_____

It's difficult for me to change because_____

_____

The one thing holding me back is_____

_____

If only I were more _____

Therefore, to be successful at turning my good intention into results, I need to:

1.   _____

2.   _____

3.   _____

Turning Good Intentions into Results

Ready . . .   Once again, check your current readiness for change. Determine if you are ready to make a commitment and stick to it. In addition to the "Therefore..." on the previous page, what else do you need to do to increase your success? Apply the formula to this specific desired change by giving yourself a score from 1 to 10, <u>1 being very low and 10 being very high</u>, on each of the following factors.

FACTORS   your SCORE from 1-10

SD = **Sufficient Dissatisfaction with the way things are now**   _____

CV = **a Clear Vision of how you want it to be in the future**   _____

KH = **the Know-How to get started; knowing what to do first**   _____

BIS = **Belief In Self; having confidence in your ability to succeed**   _____

CC = **Choice and Commitment; choosing to do it now!**

   Now total your scores: (SD + CV + KH) x BIS = CC

   ___ + ___ + ___ X ___ = ___

Which factors need to be strengthened to increase your commitment?

Therefore, I need to

   1. _____

   2. _____

   3. _____

Turning Good Intentions into Results

Take Aim . . .   List all the little, itty-bitty, easy-to-do tasks or next steps to move you toward your goal. An itty-bitty task is something you can do in 10 or 20 minutes.

_____   _____

_____   _____

_____   _____

_____   _____

_____   _____

_____   _____

Fire!   Now, act on at least one of these itty-bitty tasks each day. Don't let yourself go to sleep any night unless you have done at least one task that day. Just like baby steps, you will start down the path to your future and build momentum each day. In this way, you'll move a little closer each day to the success of making your dream a reality.

Chapter Five

Planning Your Future

"Cherish your visions and your dreams,
as they are the children of your soul,
the blueprint of your ultimate achievement."

"The key to happiness is having dreams.
The key to success is making dreams come true."

"Attitude Savers" from *Successories*

In this chapter:

- **Perspective on the Choice**

- **Pro-active Change toward your Future**

- **Planning for Your Future**

- **A Values Survey**

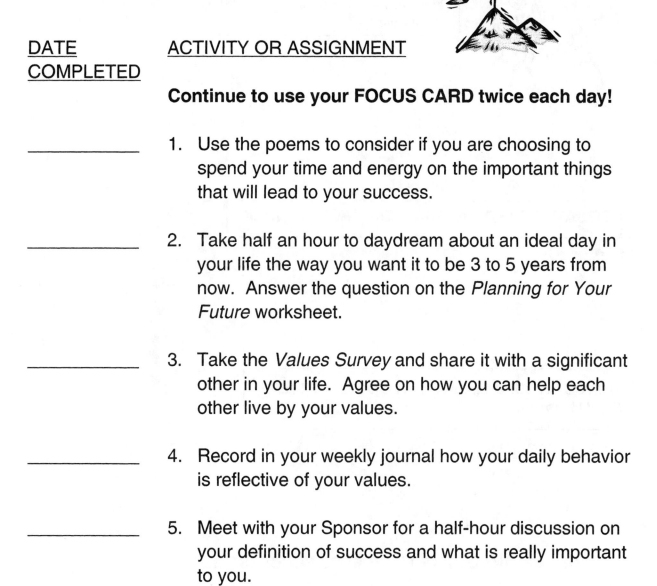

Week Five — Instruction Sheet — Planning Your Future

DATE COMPLETED	ACTIVITY OR ASSIGNMENT

Continue to use your FOCUS CARD twice each day!

_____ 1. Use the poems to consider if you are choosing to spend your time and energy on the important things that will lead to your success.

_____ 2. Take half an hour to daydream about an ideal day in your life the way you want it to be 3 to 5 years from now. Answer the question on the *Planning for Your Future* worksheet.

_____ 3. Take the *Values Survey* and share it with a significant other in your life. Agree on how you can help each other live by your values.

_____ 4. Record in your weekly journal how your daily behavior is reflective of your values.

_____ 5. Meet with your Sponsor for a half-hour discussion on your definition of success and what is really important to you.

Weekly Journal

SUCCESS I HAVE CREATED THIS WEEK:
(What did I accomplish this week that had a significant positive impact?)

SITUATIONS I FOUND CHALLENGING THIS WEEK:

THINGS I WOULD LIKE TO HAVE DONE BETTER:
(What I learned...)

ACTIONS I PLAN TO TAKE TO BE MORE SUCCESSFUL:

1. _____

2. _____

3. _____

4. _____

5. _____

Perspective on Choice

This is the beginning of a new day.
God has given me this day to use as I will.
I can waste it or use it for good.
But what I do today is very, very important,
  for I am exchanging a day of my life for it.
When tomorrow comes, this day will be gone forever,
  leaving something in its place that I have traded for it.
I want it to be gain not loss, good not evil, success
  not failure,
In order that I shall not forget the price I paid for it.

Today is a treasure given to me in the
  same quantity of seconds, minutes and
  hours that are given to others.
I am determined not to waste time worrying
  about what might happen, but to invest
  my time in making things happen.
I will not think of what might be done if I were
  different; I'm not different. I will do with
  what I have.
I will not say, "If I could find the time," because
  I will not find the time for anything. If I
  want the time, I will have to make it.
I will begin by doing, and not wasting the precious
  time I have. I will seek to improve myself--
  for I will be needed and I must not be found
  wanting.

PRO-ACTIVE Change
Toward Your Future

You have the gift of choice. You can choose how you respond to changes that happen in your life. If fact, you have the "respond-ability" to take whatever happens and make the best of it. You cannot always control the situations or the other people in your life, but you can control how you react to them. Because no one can make you feel discouraged unless you let them. No one can make you feel angry unless you let them. No one can make you give up on your hopes and dreams unless you let them. And you can choose not to let others determine your future.

You also have the gift of choice and the responsibility to plan your life the way you would like it to be, rather than just let it happen to you. It starts with a dream of the future, a vision in your mind of how you want to live your life in the years to come, an image of how you want to look, to feel, and to act, that brings you great joy and satisfaction.

It is easy to get so caught up in responding to the little things you have to do on a daily basis that you don't make the time to dream about your future—the way you want it to be—and turn those dreams into exciting visions, the visions into plans, and the plans into actions. You either make life happen for you, or you just let life happen to you.

A basic principal in psychology is that *you move toward what you picture*. If what you picture for your life is what you have right now, then you get more of the same. That is okay, unless you want things to get better. So if you picture being healthier, happier, and more successful, then your mind will automatically search out opportunities for you to move toward your vision. As you discover the opportunities to a brighter future, you need the self-confidence and willpower to act on those opportunities. This is where the new habit of being pro-active comes in handy. "It is like me to see and take advantage of opportunities that move me toward my vision of the future." You become like the person you imagine yourself to be.

Start using your gift of choice and your power of vision to be pro-active at making your life the best it can be.

Let me tell you a story about how this concept changed my life.

Example: While working with Dr. Herb Sheppard, the Organization Development Consultant for my employer, I experienced a planning strategy for helping people with Life and Career Management. It happened at a time when I was dissatisfied with my current job and uncertain about what I really wanted to do when I grew up. Dr. Sheppard asked me to move ahead in my mind to a time that was three to five years in the future. He asked me to imagine a typical day in my life the way I wanted it to be. Not a vacation day, but a regular working day. Imagine waking up in the morning, and hour-by-hour, until I went to bed at night, what did I picture? He encouraged me to take my time creating this vision. He told me not to worry about whether it was possible, or how I would achieve it, but to let my values and needs determine my fantasy of the ideal day.

Well, I created the most wonderful daydream. I imagined owning my own business, traveling all over the world at someone else's expense, giving motivational talks, teaching groups of people self-management skills, and helping individuals plan their future. I imagined a wonderful loving relationship with my wife and children. I could even picture a big house full of kids that we were helping to adjust to life's challenges. I pictured myself, trim, fit, and full of energy. It was an inspiring vision I would dream about over and over again.

With this clear sense of direction, I began to see opportunities I had never seen before, and I began to be pro-active at changing me, my habits, and my attitudes to move me toward that dream. It didn't take three years or even five years for my vision of the ideal day to become a reality; it actually took seven years. But what a wonderful journey it has been!

It is scary to think about where I would be today, if I had simply let life happen to me rather than make life happen for me.   Once you have a vision of your future, it provides a sense of direction for your decisions. Once you fall in love with that dream, it provides the motivation to make it happen. Once you make a commitment to your future, it provides the reason to change your habits to act in ways that will allow you to be successful in achieving your goals.

Planning for Your Future

"We move toward what we picture.
We become like the person we imagine ourselves to be."

CREATE a picture of how you want your life to be three to five years from now. Use your gift of imagination and day-dream about a typical *ideal* day in your life, the way would like it to be, from waking up in the morning, through each hour of the day, until you go to sleep at night. You may have several versions of this ideal day. Be as specific as you can about the details. After you have created your fantasy of the ideal day, try to answer some of the following questions.

Where are you living? How are you living? What is your quality of life?

How do you look? How do you feel? How are you dressed?

What kind of relationship do you have with your family and friends?

What are you accomplishing in your career? How are you spending your time?

What are you doing for recreation and fun?

A Values Survey
Is your fantasy consistent with your values?

DIRECTIONS: *Check* any values that you feel are important to you.
Add additional things you value on the following page.
Rank order your top ten values.

_____   1.)   **Achievement (sense of accomplishment, mastery of skills)**

_____   2.)   **Advancement (promotion, status)**

_____   3.)   **Adventure (new and challenging experiences)**

_____   4.)   **Affection (love, caring relationships)**

_____   5.)   **Competitiveness (winning, taking risks)**

_____   6.)   **Cooperation (working well with others, teamwork)**

_____   7.)   **Creativity (being imaginative, innovative)**

_____   8.)   **Economic Security (steady, adequate income)**

_____   9.)   **Fame (being famous, well-known)**

_____   10.)   **Family Happiness (time to enjoy family togetherness)**

_____   11.)   **Freedom (independence, autonomy)**

_____   12.)   **Friendship (close relationships with others)**

_____   13.)   **Health (being physically and mentally well)**

_____   14.)   **Helpfulness (assisting others, improving society)**

_____   15.)   **Inner Harmony (being at peace with yourself)**

_____   16.)   **Integrity (honesty, sincerity, standing up for beliefs)**

_____   17.)   **Involvement (participating with others, belonging)**

_____   18.)   **Loyalty (duty, respectfulness, obedience)**

_____   19.)   **Order (organized, stability, conformity)**

_____   20.)   **Personal Development (use of talent and potential)**

A Values Survey
continued

What is really important?

_____   21.)   **Pleasure (fun, laughs, leisurely lifestyle)**

_____   22.)   **Power (control, authority, influence over others)**

_____   23.)   **Recognition (respect from others, appreciation)**

_____   24.)   **Religion (spirituality, closeness to God)**

_____   25.)   **Responsibility (reliable, accountability for results)**

_____   26.)   **Self-Respect (liking yourself, pride, personal identity)**

_____   27.)   **Wealth (making money, being rich)**

_____   28.)   **Wisdom (understanding life, discovering knowledge)**

Add some of your own values:

29.)   _____

30.)   _____

31.)   _____

32.)   _____

Rank Order: *List the top ten items in order of their importance to you.*

(1) _____   (6) _____

(2) _____   (7) _____

(3) _____   (8) _____

(4) _____   (9) _____

(5) _____   (10) _____

What do you need to change to live your life in a manner that is consistent with your values?

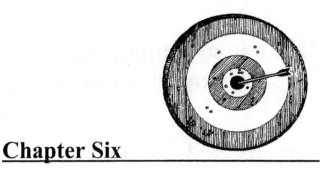

Chapter Six

<u>Clarifying Purpose and Direction</u>

"The work to be done, the goal you seek, will be achieved only when you get off dead center and make a start."

Wilferd A. Peterson, <u>The New Book of the Art of Living</u>

"You become successful the moment you start moving toward a worthwhile goal."

"Attitude Savers" from *Successories*

<u>**In this chapter:**</u>

- ❑ **Clarifying Purpose and Direction**

- ❑ **Keys to Effective Goal-Setting**

Week Six Instruction Sheet
Clarifying Purpose and Direction

DATE
COMPLETED

ACTIVITY OR ASSIGNMENT

Continue to use your FOCUS CARD twice each day!

_____ 1. Summarize what you have decided about the direction for your life by writing your personal mission statement, with your vision, values, goals, and objectives.

_____ 2. Check your goals against the 12 guidelines of *Keys to Effective Goal-Setting*.

_____ 3. Record in your weekly journal your successes.

_____ 4. Meet with your Sponsor for a half-hour discussion on how your personal and professional goals can help you achieve your mission and vision.

Weekly Journal

SUCCESS I HAVE CREATED THIS WEEK:
(What did I accomplish this week that had a significant positive impact?)

SITUATIONS I FOUND CHALLENGING THIS WEEK:

THINGS I WOULD LIKE TO HAVE DONE BETTER:
(What I learned...)

ACTIONS I PLAN TO TAKE TO BE MORE SUCCESSFUL:

1. _____

2. _____

3. _____

4. _____

5. _____

Clarifying Purpose and Direction
for My Life

A MISSION is the purpose or reason for existence—what you are all about.

My Personal Mission Statement:

_____

_____

_____

A VISION is a clear, sensory-rich, detailed mental image or picture of the way you want things to be at some point in the future—a dream put into action.

In the future, I see myself as:

_____

_____

_____

_____

A VALUE is something you believe is very important, desirable, and worthy of high regard. Values affect your choices in life.

My top ten values are:

_____   _____

_____   _____

_____   _____

_____   _____

_____   _____

Clarifying Purpose and Direction
for My Life
continued

A GOAL is something you want to achieve—a sought-after accomplishment or level of performance.

My goals for this next year are:

_____

_____

_____

_____

_____

_____

An OBJECTIVE is a specific description of what you will do to achieve the goal. It describes:

- ❑ **actions or behaviors that will be performed;**
- ❑ **conditions under which they will be performed;**
- ❑ **criteria for measuring the results.**

My objectives for the next six weeks are:

_____

_____

_____

_____

_____

_____

_____

_____

_____

Clarifying Purpose and Direction
for My Life
continued

ACTION STEPS are the sequence of tasks to be performed to accomplish the objectives and serve as a "to do" list to move you toward the goals. Some of these action steps could be the itty-bitty tasks that can be done in 10 or 20 minutes to build momentum for turning good intentions into results.

Some action steps needed to accomplish the objectives are:

_____

_____

_____

_____

_____

_____

_____

_____

_____

_____

An **ACTION PLAN** details the who, what, when, where, why, and how of the action steps. It may be needed for more complex actions involving more than one person, such as a plan to move to a new house. It assigns deadlines, lists resources, plans how to deal with obstacles, and plans rewards for the accomplishment. It is a tool for accountability and keeping people focused and productive.

Sample:

ACTION	WHO	WHAT	WHEN	WHERE	HOW

<u>Keys To Effective Goal-Setting</u>

1.   **Get The Big Picture = balanced improvement in many areas of life, with goals for being well-rounded, healthy, happy, and successful.**

2.   **Order and Consistency = goals that are leading you in the same general direction.**

3.   **Cooperation and Teamwork = help, support, and encouragement from significant others.**

4.   **Constructive Images = see what you want, instead of seeing what you want to avoid.**

5.   **Clear Images = specific, definable achievements that give you a clear picture of success.**

6.   **Accomplished End Results = see the end rewards and feel the joy of success.**

7.   **Accountability = "If it is to be, it is up to me!" Identify specific actions that lead to success.**

8.   **General Time Frames = avoid unrealistic time limits that put pressure on you and increase the possibility of failure.**

9.   **Confidentiality = share your goals only with those who can help you accomplish them.**

10.   **On-going Change = when you near the achievement of one goal, set another one to keep momentum.**

11.   **Write Goals Down = give yourself a specific thing to look at and focus on everyday.**

12.   **Imagination = vividly envision the achievement of your goals.**

Adapted from the work of Lou Tice in his workbook,
Building Your Business by Achieving Your Potential

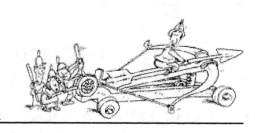

Chapter Seven

Evaluation and Next Steps

"The sky is the limit when your heart is in it."

"Some succeed because they are destined to.
Most succeed because they are determined to."

"Attitude Savers" from *Successories*

<u>**In this chapter:**</u>

❑ **Evaluation of Sponsorship Process**

❑ **Creating New Focus Cards**

❑ **Conditions for Future Job Success**

❑ **You Are a Magical Creature**

Week Seven Instruction Sheet
Evaluation & Next Steps

DATE COMPLETED	ACTIVITY OR ASSIGNMENT

Continue to use your FOCUS CARDS periodically to reinforce your new habits.

_____ 1. Complete the evaluation form and share it with your Sponsor, so you can learn how to improve your results in the future. In order to improve the sponsorship process for everyone, please FAX a copy of your evaluation form to PATH Associates at 410-821-0538. Thank you.

_____ 2. Choose another personal behavior and another professional behavior you want to change in order to continue moving toward your vision of the ideal day. Start the six-week process again, creating new FOCUS CARDS. Use this process for continued growth and improvement.

_____ 3. Determine what needs to change in your current job or career situation that will allow you to do your very best. Complete the worksheet on *Conditions for Future Success.* Discuss the conditions with your immediate boss to determine how these conditions could be created to permit improved performance on the job.

_____ 4. Read *You Are A Magical Creature,* and choose to become a Sponsor for someone else by helping him or her learn how to take control of their success.

Weekly Journal

SUCCESS I HAVE CREATED THIS WEEK:
(What did I accomplish this week that had a significant positive impact?)

SITUATIONS I FOUND CHALLENGING THIS WEEK:

THINGS I WOULD LIKE TO HAVE DONE BETTER:
(What I learned...)

ACTIONS I PLAN TO TAKE TO BE MORE SUCCESSFUL:

1. _____

2. _____

3. _____

4. _____

5. _____

Evaluation of Sponsorship Process

Answer questions 1to 5 using a SCALE of 1 (very low) to 7 (very high). Then honestly respond to questions 6-9.

1. **At the start of this process, what was your level of understanding, buy-in, and belief in this method of behavior change for performance improvement?** _____

2. **What has been your level of commitment to apply the process on a daily basis? Have you used your FOCUS CARD every day?** _____

3. **What level of success have you experienced in modifying your behavior?**

    Professional Goal _____

    Personal Goal _____

4. **What degree of difficulty did you experienced in using this process of personal growth?** _____

5. **What is the likelihood that you would continue to use this method for creating improved habits in the future?** _____

6. **What was most helpful to you in using this process?**

7. **What was the least helpful to you in using this process?**

8. **What do you recommend to improve this process?**

9. **What suggestions do you have for implementing the Sponsorship Model with others?**

Creating New Focus Cards
How to continue to develop improved habits

How it's done   Changing or reshaping your habits is a process of reprogramming your beliefs and expectations about you. As you develop a new picture of how you act, the behaviors will change to become consistent with your new self-image.

Step 1   From your list in chapter one of characteristics or habits you want to develop, choose another professional goal and another personal goal to work on during the next six weeks.

top of
the card   *example: Become a "do it now" person.* (avoid procrastination)

Step 2   List WHY it is important to you to make this behavior change. Determine the intensity of your desire to change. List what it will do for you and how it will make you feel to have this new habit.

front of   *Avoid penalties for being late*   *Improve reputation with others*
the card
              Stop missing great opportunities   *Get things done on time*

              Less stress & last-minute rushing   *Personal satisfaction*

Step 3   Now write a one-sentence description of what your behavior looks like and how it feels to naturally act in accordance with your desired habit.

front of
the card   I choose to be a "do it now" person who does what needs to be done, when it ought to be done, whether I like it or not.

              It is like me to take care of things immediately and get them finished promptly.

              It is becoming easier for me to make decisions quickly and confidently.

              I am good at meeting deadlines and keeping appointments.

Creating New Focus Cards

Step 4   List any specific behaviors you will need to change to be successful. What will you need to start or stop doing? Write a one-sentence description of yourself doing those things easily, effortlessly, and naturally.

back of
the card   **I am self-disciplined and stay focused on getting the important things done.**

I am organized, so I know what needs to be done and do it.

I feel in control of my life and make the best use of my time.

I get started quickly and work efficiently.

It is like me to do things even if I don't enjoy them, because I want the long-term benefit.

Step 5   Use the FOCUS CARD everyday to imprint the new image into your sub-conscious mind. To do this, follow these simple directions:

✓ Read the FOCUS CARD, front and back.

✓ Close your eyes. Visualize exactly what you're saying and doing.

✓ Feel how good it is to have the desired quality and habit.

✓ Repeat this process twice each day, first thing in the morning when you wake up and last thing in the evening before going to sleep. Do this everyday, seven days a week, for 4 to 6 weeks, and make the new behavior a habit.

Conditions for Future Job Success
How to negotiate with your boss

The Concept

Everyone is capable of improved performance, under the right conditions. That means, if you can change some things about your work situation, you could be more effective, efficient, and productive. The challenge is to find a way to negotiate with your boss and management to help you make those changes that will allow you to improve your daily performance. It is in your boss's best interest to help you make these changes, since management's job is to obtain the very best work performance from each and every employee.

Your choice

If you choose to take responsibility for your job and career success, you may want to use this strategy to improve your current job situation. It is best to approach your boss with the idea that you take pride in doing a good job and assume that your boss wants you to do your very best work. Because you know yourself better than anyone else, you know the conditions under which you can be most creative, productive and successful. You would like to share some of these conditions with your boss in the hope that he or she would be willing to help you look at how those conditions might be created. The secret is to be reasonable in your requests and suggest simple ways to implement the changes. The return on the investment of your boss's time and effort is that you do a better job at your job.

There is no guarantee that this will work, but essentially you have nothing to lose. By doing this, you communicate your desire to do your best work and show that you are self-confident by expressing your needs. If your current boss is not interested in helping you be successful, or the conditions for your success cannot be created, then you can use your list to start looking for a job opportunity that will allow you to be successful.

Example:

I need quiet space in which to concentrate. When our work team moved to new office space, I had to share a small cubical with two of my co-workers. When they were talking on the phone, which they did a lot, I could not keep my mind on my work. I would become distracted, frustrated, and unproductive. I just couldn't seem to tune out all of the noise the way

82

other people did. So, using this strategy, I met with my boss to discuss the conditions under which I was willing and able to do my best work. He could not provide me with my own office space. However, he suggested that when I needed quiet space to work, that I move to the reference library just down the hall. He would set up a desk in the library for my use. This negotiated agreement worked out very well. What I learned is that I had to take responsibility for creating my own success and could not expect my boss to know what I needed.

Your Responsibility	**To identify and communicate the specific conditions that enable you to achieve success by using your time, talent, and skill to consistently perform to the best of your abilities.**
Management's Responsibility	**To work with each and every employee to create, as much as possible, the CONDITIONS under which the employees can do their best work.**
Work Team's Responsibility	**To work together to help create and maintain the best working conditions for everyone, taking into account the organizational goals and resource limitations, as well as each person's unique behavior style.**

Success in my job = _____

_____

_____

Identifying Conditions for Success

List the Conditions under which you would be both willing and able to do your very best work.	*Describe how these conditions might be created and the impact of these changes on you and others.*
i.e., Periods of uninterrupted time to concentrate on doing my work	*Quiet hours = Agreed upon times to minimize interruptions*
Being kept well-informed of changes	*Frequent emails or daily meetings*
Occasional positive feedback	*Notes about what I have done well*
Understanding <u>why</u> a task is important	*Delegate by giving full information*

<u>Identifying Your Conditions for Success</u>

***List the Conditions* under which you would be both *willing* and *able* to do your very best work.**

***Describe how* these conditions might be created and the impact of these changes on you and others.**

You Are A Magical Creature

If you tell someone they are wonderful—
capable of magic,
a small spark—
maybe a chemical reaction of hope—
jumps the synapse of skepticism
about self and world,
and creates a new combustion,
capable of generating
magic and hope in others.
If only we would go around—
honestly and sincerely
proclaiming each other's wonderfulness,
more capacity could be released
than any realist would ever dare believe.
The shy leaping moment
when a person
thinks, feels, believes
against all odds
that he or she can make a difference
is the beginning of transformation,
not only of the self
but of the entire society.

—Sharon L. Connelly

References and Resources
for Success Management

Staying Healthy   <u>The Joy of Stress: How to Make Stress Work for You</u> by Peter Hanson, M.D. Andrews and McMeel, 1991.

<u>Spontaneous Healing</u> by Andrew Weil, M.D. Ballantine Books, 1995.

Options for Change   <u>Choices</u> by Shad Helmsetter, Ph.D. Simon & Schuster, 1989.

<u>Don't Sweat the Small Stuff . . . and It's All Small Stuff</u> by Richard Carlson, Ph.D. Hyperion, 1997.

<u>Emotional Intelligence</u> by Daniel Goleman. Bantam Books, 1995.

Changing Self   <u>The Self-Talk Solution</u> by Shad Helmsetter, Ph.D. Simon & Schuster, 1987.

<u>Creative Visualization</u> by Shakti Gawain. Bantam Books, 1978.

Changing Habits   <u>The 7 Habits of Highly Effective People</u> by Stephen R. Covey. Simon & Schuster, 1989.

<u>Kicking Your Stress Habits: A Do-it-Yourself Guide for Coping with Stress</u> by Donald A. Tubesing, Ph.D. Signet Books, 1982.

<u>21 Days To A Healthy 21st Century Attitude</u> by Mary Kay Kurzweg, 1999.

Time Management   <u>First Things First</u> by Stephen R. Covey, A. Roger Merrill, Rebecca R. Merrill. Simon & Schuster, 1994.

<u>How to Get Control of Your Time and Your Life</u> by Alan Lakein. A Signet Book, 1973.

About PATH Associates

The author, Bob Younglove, is the co-founder and President of PATH Associates, an international consulting firm specializing in performance improvement strategies.

The *mission* of PATH Associates is
> to help people take responsible actions in their lives
>> to be healthier, happier, and more successful in
>>> achieving their goals.

To accomplish this mission, PATH Associates offers the following services:
- Motivational keynote talks at association conferences, management retreats, and organization meetings.
- Practical workshops that teach strategies for self-management and dealing with people in difficult situations.
- Humorous advice on maintaining emotional control given through stories, books, and articles.
- Performance coaching with individuals and teams on how to change behaviors to be more successful in sports, careers, and relationships.
- Community Outreach Programs for parents, teachers, coaches, and youth leaders in how to positively influence children and teens.

For more information on how PATH Associates can help you,
visit our web site at PATHassociatesonline.com,
or call our office in the United States at 410-821-0538.

If you have questions about how to effectively use the concepts and strategies in SPONSOR SUCCESS, or need help in achieving your success, email Bob Younglove at PATHassoc@AOL.com.

Consider how you can be a sponsor of success for a friend, a family member, or a co-worker. Order a SPONSOR SUCCESS book as a gift that can truly make a difference in their quality of life. Show your love and concern by expressing your wish and belief for their health, happiness, and success.

GIFT BOOK ORDER FORM

> I would like to order copies of this self-help book, *SPONSOR SUCCESS: A Workbook for Turning Good Intentions into Results* as a gift for my family and friends.

Please send copies to:

name_____   name_____

address_____   address_____

_____   _____

name_____   name_____

address_____   address_____

_____   _____

*Please enclose a gift card from*_____

Contact Information: your name_____

your address _____

_____

your phone # _____

Payment Method: **Credit card**☐   **Check**☐   **Money Order**☐

Type of card _____ $15.95 each book X ___ = [   ]

Card Number_____   Maryland residents add

Expiration date_____   5% sales tax   = [   ]

Name on card_____   Shipping: $4.75 per book

$1 for each additional book [   ]

Signature   _____

Total [   ]

How to order:

- ☐ **Fax completed order form to PATH Associates at <u>410-821-0538</u>**
- ☐ **Mail to PATH Associates   OR   Call American Literary Press**
  19 Coldwater Court   <u>410-882-7700</u>
  Towson, MD 21204-2044
- ☐ **Email** PATHassoc@AOL.com   **Amerlit@erols.com**

ORGANIZATIONAL BOOK ORDER FORM

> **I would like to order copies of *SPONSOR SUCCESS:*
> *A Workbook for Turning Good Intentions into Results*
> for my work group, team, department, or organization.**

Name _____Title _____

Organization _____

Address _____Phone #_____

City _____State_____Zip_____Country_____

_____Number of copies to be shipped to _____

Organization _____

Address _____Phone #_____

City _____State_____Zip_____Country_____

Please contact American Literary Press for information on discount pricing and shipping, by calling 410-882-7700 or email them at amerlit@erols.com

Payment Method: Credit card☐   Check☐   Money Order☐

Type of card _____ $15.95 each book X ___ = [   ]
Card Number_____   Maryland residents add
Expiration date_____   5% sales tax   = [   ]
Name on card_____   Shipping: $4.75 per book [   ]
                                       $1 for each additional book
Signature _____

                                       Total   [   ]

How to order:
  ❑ **Fax completed order form to PATH Associates at <u>410-821-0538</u>**
  ❑ **Mail to PATH Associates   <u>OR</u> Call American Literary Press**
     19 Coldwater Court   <u>410-882-7700</u>
     Towson, MD 21204-2044
  ❑ **Email <u>PATHassoc@AOL.com</u>   Amerlit@erols.com**